Ancient Civilizations

Published by Creative Education
P.O. Box 227, Mankato, Minnesota 56002
Creative Education is an imprint of
THE CREATIVE COMPANY
www.thecreativecompany.us

Design and production by CHRISTINE VANDERBEEK
Art direction by RITA MARSHALL

Printed in the United States of America

PHOTOGRAPHS BY Alamy (dieKleinert, North Wind
Picture Archives), Corbis (Peter Essick/Aurora Photos,
Macduff Everton, Kevin Fleming, Kenneth Garrett/
National Geographic Society, Historical Picture Archive,
National Geographic Society, Alfredo Dagli Orti/
The Art Archive, Gianni Dagli Orti), iStockphoto
(pchoui, TonyBraggett), Shutterstock (Moreno Novello),
SuperStock (Album/Oronoz/Album, DeAgostini, David
Hiser/National Geographic, Image Asset Management
Ltd., SuperStock)

LIBRARY OF CONGRESS
CATALOGING-IN-PUBLICATION DATA
Bodden, Valerie.
Aztec empire / Valerie Bodden.
p. cm. — (Ancient civilizations)
Includes bibliographical references and index.
SUMMARY: A historical overview of the Aztec civilization
from the perspectives of the social classes, from the no-
bles to the commoners, including the Mexican empire's
growth and decline.

ISBN 978-1-60818-390-6
1. Aztecs—Juvenile literature. I. Title.

F1219.73.B64 2014
972—dc23   2013032507

CCSS: RI.5.1, 2, 3, 5, 6, 8, 9; RH.6-8.4, 5, 6, 7, 8, 9

FIRST EDITION
9 8 7 6 5 4 3 2 1

CREATIVE C EDUCATION

AZTEC EMPIRE

VALERIE BODDEN

Aztec Empire

TABLE OF CONTENTS

INTRODUCTION

According to legend, a beautiful land known as Aztlan was once the home of a group of people known as the Mexica (*meh-SHE-kuh*). The Mexica eventually left Aztlan, though, and traveled south for many generations. Along the way, they settled temporarily in several locations, until, around 1325, they came to an island on Lake Texcoco. There, the Mexica saw an eagle sitting on a cactus, eating a snake. They believed this was a sign from their god Huitzilopochtli that the island would be their permanent home.

Lake Texcoco was located on a large, high ***plateau*** known as the Valley of Mexico. The 3,000-square-mile (7,770 sq km) valley was surrounded by high mountains.

An illustration from a 1579 Spanish book shows the legendary founding of Tenochtitlan.

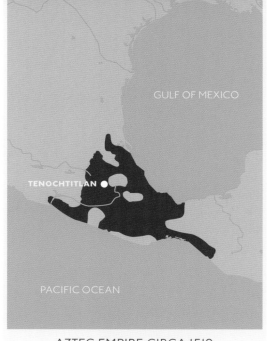

TENOCHTITLAN ●

PACIFIC OCEAN

AZTEC EMPIRE CIRCA 1519

Lake Texcoco was part of a chain of shallow lakes near the center of the valley. The region's fertile soils and many lakes had drawn people to farm and live on the land for more than 6,500 years before the Mexica arrived. Some of those peoples—such as the Toltecs, who flourished from A.D. 950 to 1150—had developed rich customs, many of which the Mexica eventually adopted.

The Mexica named their island home Tenochtitlan, meaning "Place of the Cactus Fruit." The island was surrounded by numerous small city-states. Each city-state consisted of a powerful city along with the surrounding countryside. Tenochtitlan soon became one of the most powerful city-states. In 1428, Tenochtitlan allied with the city-states of Texcoco and Tlacopan to form an empire known as the Triple Alliance. By the early 1500s, the Triple Alliance ruled over 5 or 6 million people in the Valley of Mexico and beyond. Today, the term "Aztec" is often used to refer to the Mexica as well as the numerous peoples over whom they ruled. The empire of the Triple Alliance is often referred to as simply the Aztec Empire.

Life in the Aztec Empire was sharply divided into two groups, or social classes. The nobles, known as *pipiltin*, ruled the empire and its various city-states. They served as priests and commanded the army. The rest of Aztec civilization was made up of commoners, or *macehualtin*. Commoners farmed the land, made crafts, or engaged in trade. They paid **tribute** and provided service to the nobles. Strict laws regulated the privileges enjoyed by nobles and denied to commoners. Even so, with hard work, successful commoners could improve their position in society. They could enjoy some advantages denied to other commoners. But there would always be a divide between them and the true nobility.

The Aztec Empire, even at its height in 1519, was not a continuous territory of lands.

TLACATECUHTLI   TEQUIHUA

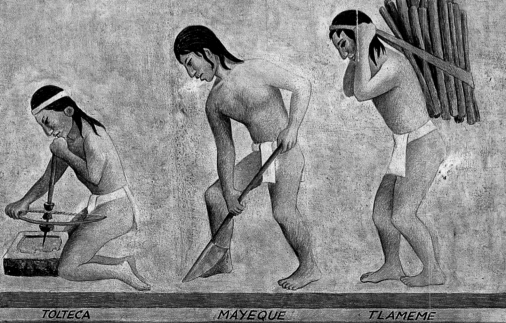

TOLTECA   MAYEQUE   TLAMEME

PRIVILEGED PIPILTIN

Each of the numerous city-states that dotted the Valley of Mexico was ruled by a *tlatoani*, or king. All the land in the city-state was owned or controlled by the tlatoani, who received tribute from the people of the city-state. In return, the tlatoani protected the people. He was their leader in battle and participated in religious ceremonies to appease the gods.

When the Mexica first settled at Tenochtitlan, they were not strong enough to establish an independent city-state with its own tlatoani. Instead, they allied themselves with the Tepanec city-state. In return for the protection of the Tepanecs, the Mexica provided tribute, usually in the form of military service. Around

Later Aztec emperors such as Moctezuma II (1466–1520) came out of the tlatoani tradition.

the year 1372, Tenochtitlan installed a tlatoani of its own. His power was limited by Tenochtitlan's relationship with the Tepanecs, though.

By 1428, the Mexica were ready to be independent. With help from the people of Texcoco and Tlacopan, they defeated the Tepanecs and established the Triple Alliance, an empire that ruled over the other city-states in the Valley of Mexico. The tlatoani of Tenochtitlan soon became the major power in the new empire. He was given the title *huey tlatoani*, or "great speaker." Today, we call him emperor of the Aztecs. Although the emperor was at the top of the social pyramid, other *tlatoque* (the plural form of *tlatoani*) continued to govern their city-states, as long as they sent tribute to Tenochtitlan.

The position of emperor was not necessarily passed down from father to son. When an emperor died, a council of his male relatives selected his successor. They could choose any male from the royal family. Often, the successor chosen was the deceased emperor's brother,

Did You Know?

TO APPROACH THE EMPEROR, NOBLES HAD TO REMOVE THEIR DECORATED CLOAKS AND SANDALS AND WALK WITH THEIR EYES LOOKING DOWN; THEY WALKED BACKWARDS WHEN THEY LEFT.

son, nephew, or grandson. Once a new ruler had been selected, he had to participate in several rituals before taking the throne. These rituals involved making religious offerings, *fasting*, and leading a battle to capture victims for human sacrifice. For the coronation ceremony itself, nobles from other city-states were invited to Tenochtitlan, where they were entertained with theatrical presentations, music, and dancing.

Once the new emperor took the throne, he relied on other members of the pipiltin, or noble class, to help with the administration of the government. Just below the emperor was the office of the *cihuacoatl*, who saw to the day-to-day aspects of governing and served as ruler when the emperor was away. Below the cihuacoatl were high-ranking nobles known as *tetecuhtin* (singular *tecuhtli*). The tetecuhtin were given estates by the tlatoani and were allowed to collect any income generated by those estates as well as tribute from the commoners who worked the land. Other nobles served as government ministers or ambassadors.

The election of an emperor was an occasion that called for great ceremony.

matcaquan e illapena litt
liene poa poa poa lapecida
ll pana maria 2 tea len
gian. ccia tsi eslaua da

Did You Know?

———

TENOCHTITLAN WAS

LAID OUT IN AN ORDER-

LY GRID PATTERN AND

KEPT CLEAN THROUGH

GARBAGE COLLECTION,

STREET CLEANING, AND

THE USE OF PUBLIC

BATHROOMS.

———

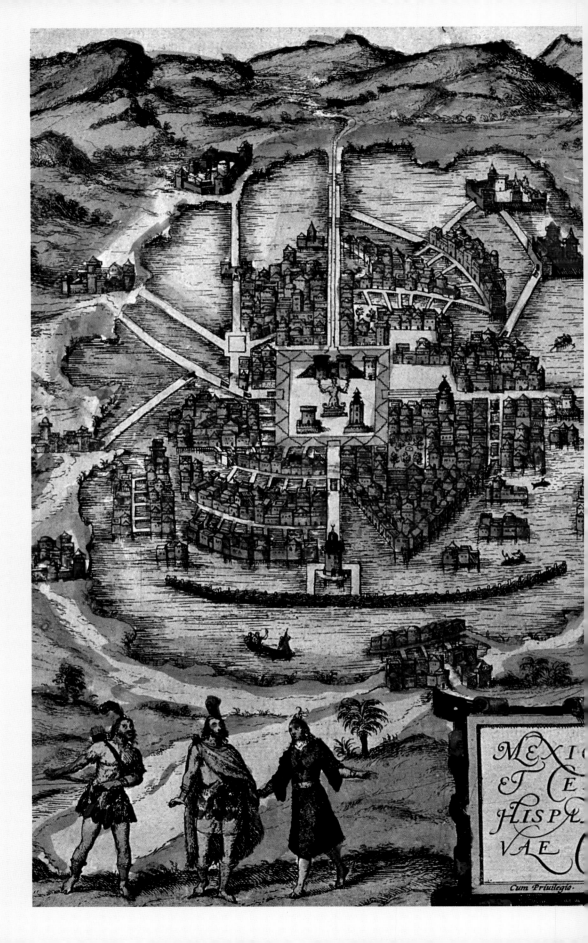

Nobles believed they were descendants of the first Mexica tlatoani. Thus, membership in the nobility was hereditary, and nobles enjoyed a number of special privileges. For example, they could own land and collect tribute. It was against the law for anyone but nobles to live in a two-story home or to wear cotton clothing.

In addition, the children of a nobleman were educated at a special school, known as a *calmecac*. Education began between the ages of 6 and 10. Both boys and girls from noble families went to school, although they attended separate calmecac. For boys, education was aimed at producing future priests, warriors, and government leaders. Training included religion, music and dance, military arts, history, law, and reading and writing. Boys also learned methods of self-control and discipline. They were forced to sleep on hard stone floors, bathe in icy ponds, and get up in the middle of the night to carry out ceremonies. They participated in construction projects such as digging canals. They ate little—sometimes only three tortillas and a bowl of water in a day.

While boys were preparing to become warriors, priests, or officials, noble girls used their time at the calmecac to prepare for their future domestic role. They were taught how to manage a household, oversee servants, and weave cloth. Some were also taught to serve as temple helpers.

Most girls were married before the age of 15—some as young as 10 or 12. Their husbands were usually in their early 20s. Nobles always married nobles; they did not intermarry with commoners. In many cases, a nobleman would marry a noblewoman from another city-state in order to secure alliances, or political partnerships, between two city-states or families. Nobles also practiced polygamy; a nobleman could marry as many wives as he chose, as long as he could provide for all of them. Each wife's status with her husband was based on her place in society before marriage.

Although noblewomen had servants and attendants to take care of the cooking and household chores, they still spent their time in productive labor. Like all other women, noblewomen spent much of their day weaving cloth, which was a source of wealth that could be used to purchase items in the market. A few women also served as doctors, and some unmarried women were priestesses.

Nobles and their wives lived in luxurious houses and palaces. While some lived in the countryside, many of the grandest homes were built in the Aztec capital of Tenochtitlan. Two roads—one running north and south, the other going east and west—split this island city into four sections and connected it to the mainland via *causeways*. The roads came together at the center of the city. This area was built up with enormous

Approximately 200,000 people lived in Tenochtitlan when the Spanish arrived in 1519.

temples and emperors' palaces. Just outside the city center were the homes of the nobles.

Each Aztec emperor built a new palace when he was crowned. These palaces could be huge complexes consisting of living quarters, courthouses, armories, libraries, and more. In addition to the emperor's family, the palace might house military leaders, scholars, advisers, and artisans. Palaces were constructed of stone and opened onto a central courtyard. Decorative curtains of cloth or feathers hung in the doorways. Exotic gardens covered the grounds—and often the rooftop. Some emperors also kept a small zoo containing such animals as birds, jaguars, monkeys, bears, and more.

Although the homes of other nobles were not as large as the emperor's palace, they were still impressive structures. Many were two stories high, and they were made of stone or *adobe*. Like the palaces, they opened onto a central courtyard, giving the family privacy. Interior walls were often covered with sweet-smelling woods such as

cedar, and statues decorated the hallways.

Inside their large homes and palaces, nobles lived a life of luxury. They were treated to the finest foods in the empire. Maize, or corn, was a staple for all Aztecs, and was often eaten in the form of tortillas or *tamales*. Beans were also served with nearly every meal. In addition, the nobility enjoyed meat on a regular basis, including turkey, quail, venison, lobster, and a large, hairless breed of dog. Only the nobility (along with a few elite traders and warriors) enjoyed chocolate for dessert, usually in the form of a drink. According to some records, the emperor and other top nobles were served up to 2,000 different dishes each day.

Nobles from the various city-states often gathered together for ceremonial feasts filled with delicacies. In addition to eating, they exchanged rich gifts of cloth, feathers, and jewelry. They participated in dances and religious rituals as well. Sharing in such feasts helped cement the ties between noble families.

Ruins from the ancient city of Teotihuacan probably inspired builders of Tenochtitlan.

GIVING TO THE GODS

The Aztecs worshiped as many as 200 different gods. These gods were thought to control the various stages of human life, such as birth, death, and disease. They also represented nature: there were gods of wind, rain, sun, maize, and more. Some gods were believed to be the **patrons** of workers in a specific trade or of people living in a certain neighborhood.

Despite the hundreds of gods they worshiped, the Aztecs had four main deities: Huitzilopochtli, Tlaloc, Quetzalcoatl, and Tezcatlipoca. Although the gods were believed to be invisible spirits, they were sometimes depicted in human or animal form. Huitzilopochtli was the sun god and the god of war and was often shown as a hummingbird or an eagle.

Mexica sculptures of gods are often in a seated position, as though accepting offerings.

Tlaloc was a rain god who granted fertility to crops and flowers. He was pictured wearing a mask with round eyes and large fangs. Quetzalcoatl, the god of learning and the priesthood, was depicted as a feathered serpent. The most powerful of all Aztec gods was Tezcatlipoca, the god of kings, who used his **obsidian** mirror to see everything that happened. He was sometimes drawn with the mirror in place of one foot.

Every Aztec god had at least one temple, often located at the top of a pyramid. Temple pyramids were found at the center of each city-state capital. Tenochtitlan had several pyramids within a walled area at the center of the city known as the sacred precinct. The greatest of these pyramids was the Templo Mayor, a stepped pyramid that rose eight stories into the sky. At the top of the pyramid were two temples, one to honor Huitzilopochtli, the other for Tlaloc. Inside each temple was a statue of that temple's god. The temples were where the Aztec people worshiped and carried out sacrifices to their gods.

Thousands of priests carried out the religious

rites of the Aztec Empire. Some historians believe that as many as 5,000 priests served at the Templo Mayor alone. Boys (and some girls) trained for the priesthood at the calmecac. Most priests were nobles, but occasionally a bright, promising commoner would attend the calmecac and train to become a priest. In addition to learning the rituals and **mythology** of the Aztec religion, young men training to become priests also had to participate in physically challenging exercises. They slept little, fasted frequently, bled themselves, and made difficult journeys up mountainsides to make sacrifices.

After completing their training around the age of 20, boys earned the position of *tlamacazqui*, or "giver of things." They remained single and served as priests for the rest of their lives. Females became *cihuatlamacazqui*, or "female giver of things," although they remained in service only until they married.

A priest's most important job was performing rituals. These included keeping the sacred fires of the temple burning, playing music, making

The Aztec name for a wall of skulls is *tzompantli*, such as this structure from the Templo Mayor.

Did You Know?

THE AZTECS LOOKED

UPON CHILDBIRTH AS A

BATTLE, AND WOMEN

WHO DIED WHILE

GIVING BIRTH WERE

BELIEVED TO GO TO THE

WARRIORS' HEAVEN.

offerings to the gods, and burning incense made from tree sap. In addition, priests oversaw the daily operations of the temple, including construction, sweeping, and caring for the statues of the gods. Priests also taught at the calmecac and kept written records of rituals. Some priests recorded the movement of the stars and planets, often using them to predict the future or to determine when to go to war.

An elite group of priests known as *tlenamacac*, or "fire priests," had a special role within the priesthood. These priests were responsible for carrying out human sacrifices, a major component of Aztec religion. Above the fire priests were two quetzalcoatl, or high priests, who were named after the patron god of priests.

Priests lived a devout lifestyle, committed to their religion. They prayed three times each day, and then got up at midnight to pray again. Although priests participated in ritual bathing, they did not wash or cut their hair, which might eventually hang to their waist or feet. The unwashed hair was stiff with dried blood from both sacrificial victims and themselves, as they participated in autosacrifice, or bloodletting. A priest's body was painted with a black dye that was thought to hold magical properties. It was made from rubber-tree sap, spiders, and scorpions. Many priests wore a black robe as a symbol of this severe lifestyle.

Aztec priests kept track of the calendar, which was divided into 18 months of 20 days apiece. Each month, the priests celebrated a specific ceremony. Many of the ceremonies dealt with the growth of crops. Nobles and commoners attended the ceremonies, which involved music, dancing, parades, and feasts.

The most important part of most festivals was human sacrifice. The Aztecs believed that the gods had given their own blood to create people and the world; therefore, people owed the gods a debt that could be repaid only with human blood. In addition, human blood was required to feed the gods.

Early in Aztec history, human sacrifice was carried out on a small scale, with only one victim being sacrificed at a time. In the mid-1400s, however, mass sacrifices became common. Up to 20,000 victims may have been sacrificed each year. In 1487, that many victims may have been killed in just four days for the dedication of the renovated Templo Mayor.

The victims of human sacrifice were generally soldiers captured in war. For at least one celebration a year, however, children were sacrificed to the rain god Tlaloc. The Aztecs believed that as the children and their parents cried, their tears would lead Tlaloc to provide rain for their crops.

Before the sacrificial act, victims were generally treated well. In some cases, they were treated as if they were the god himself. When the time

Fertility goddesses (left) were important to all ancient cultures, including the Aztecs.

for the sacrifice arrived, most victims—even those who had been captured—would willingly climb the steps of the Templo Mayor to reach the sacrificial stone at the top. Aztecs believed that being sacrificed to the gods was the most honorable way for a person to die. After death, they believed they would join the rising sun in the highest level of heaven.

When a victim reached the top of the pyramid, four priests grabbed him and thrust him down onto the sacrificial stone. A fifth priest, painted red and wearing a red robe, stabbed the sacrificial knife into the victim's chest. A drum beat in the background as the priest reached into the victim's chest and pulled out his still-beating heart. The priest held the heart up to the gods before putting it into a bowl. The victim was then rolled down the temple steps. At the bottom, his head was cut off and stuck onto a skull rack next to the pyramid. His arms and legs were given to

the warrior who had captured him in battle. This warrior and his family ate bits of the flesh in a ritual meal thought to honor the victim and give strength to the warrior. Although heart sacrifice was the most common form of Aztec human sacrifice, other victims were shot with arrows, burned, strangled, drowned, or starved.

While thousands of people gave up their lives every year for the gods, everyone from the emperor to commoners participated in autosacrifice, offering their own blood at various points in their lives. Usually, people cut their tongues, earlobes, or legs with sharp **maguey** thorns or obsidian blades. Autosacrifice was carried out when someone needed to ask the gods for a favor, such as making crops grow or being able to have a child. The priests took part in autosacrifice every night as a way of offering another, small payment to the gods.

Nineteenth-century depictions of Aztec human sacrifice were not entirely accurate.

CULTURE OF WAR

Warfare was a way of life for the Aztecs. From the time a baby boy was born, he was groomed for the life of a warrior. He was even given a tiny bow and arrow as a symbol of that future role.

The Aztecs went to war for two main reasons: to gain tribute or to capture victims for human sacrifice. In order to bring incredible wealth to the city of Tenochtitlan, the Aztecs often provoked other city-states to war. The emperor would send messengers to order a city-state to start paying tribute. If the city-state refused, the Aztecs would declare war. If they were victorious (and they usually were), the Aztecs demanded tribute. Depending on where the city-state was located and the goods it was best known for, that

In the Aztec culture, men were proud to become warriors and prove their worth on the battlefield.

tribute might be in the form of cotton capes, grain, feathers from tropical birds, gold, honey, or other luxury items. City-states located near the edges of the empire often provided their tribute in the form of military service to protect the empire's borders. By 1519, more than 400 city-states provided tribute or service to Tenochtitlan.

In addition to tribute, the Aztecs required huge numbers of people for human sacrifices. Sometimes warriors were captured during wars held to gain tribute. But at other times, the Aztecs fought special wars for the sole purpose of taking captives. These were known as Flower Wars because of the colorful clothing in which the warriors fought. The Aztecs and their enemies generally agreed to hold a Flower War whenever one needed victims for an upcoming sacrifice. Warriors volunteered to fight in these wars, since taking captives brought them prestige and a chance to move up in the ranks.

The Aztecs had no standing army, and all men in the empire were expected to serve when needed. If necessary, the Aztecs could raise an

Did You Know?

SCHOLARS DEBATE

WHETHER AZTLAN WAS

REAL OR MYTHICAL, BUT

THEY AGREE THAT THE

MEXICA CAME FROM

NORTHERN MEXICO OR

THE SOUTHWESTERN

UNITED STATES.

---

army of 200,000. The emperor served at the head of the army, and he joined his troops on the battlefield. The upper ranks of the military were filled by the most experienced and successful warriors. These were generally nobles, who had the advantage of advanced military training in the calmecac. Because military ranks were based on merit and skill, however, even commoners could rise to top-level positions.

Commoners learned military skills in their school, called the *telpoch-calli*. All boys—both commoners and nobles—joined their first battle around the age of 16. At first, they were not involved in the fighting but only carried weapons and supplies. They became participants in the battle around age 18. Until they took their first captive, the young men were not considered true warriors. After taking a captive, they were rewarded with a mantle, or cloak, decorated with a flower design. They could also wear special face paint. Each captive taken after that earned a warrior the right to wear a new, more elite mantle and to enjoy other privileges. A warrior who had taken two captives, for example,

Traditions unrelated to warfare were often born out of religious customs, such as "flying" from a post.

Did You Know?

———

AN AZTEC CHILD

WHO DISOBEYED HIS

PARENTS MIGHT BE

FORCED TO INHALE THE

SMOKE OF BURNING

CHILI PEPPERS.

———

could wear sandals on the battlefield.

The most elite soldiers were the Eagle and Jaguar warriors. These warriors had taken more than four prisoners of high rank. They were given grants of land and earned the right to march at the front of parades and to dine at the emperor's palace. They also wore elaborate costumes in battle. Jaguar warriors dressed in a jaguar-skin suit, with their heads sticking out of the jaguar's mouth, while Eagle warriors wore helmets shaped like eagles' heads, with their face showing through the eagle's huge beak.

While the Eagle and Jaguar warriors probably wore the most elaborate battle gear, other Aztec soldiers also dressed in splendid uniforms. High-ranking warriors were often covered in feathered *tunics* and headdresses. Under their decorative costumes, military leaders wore armor made of thick layers of quilted cotton. Lower-ranking warriors might make do with no armor and only a rough cloak or breechcloth for clothing. Many soldiers also carried shields made of wood or animal hide. Shields of the upper ranks were decorated with feathers, gold, or stones such as turquoise.

The Aztecs' main weapons were spears and swords. In fact, the Aztecs may have been the first peoples in the Americas to use swords. The Aztec sword, or *maquauhuitl*, was made of a long, wooden handle from which several small, sharp obsidian blades projected on each side. The blades were sharp enough to cut the head off a soldier (or, later, the horses of the Spaniards) in a single stroke. Warriors also used slings, bows and arrows, dart-throwers called *atlatls*, and clubs.

Aztec battles followed specific rules and rituals. Most battles were fought in late fall, winter, and early spring to avoid conflicts with the duties of farmers who also served as soldiers. Smaller battles, such as Flower Wars, were fought anytime. Before beginning a war, the Aztecs had to conduct negotiations with the enemy. These negotiations might include a request for tribute; the denial of such a request was considered an insult and a reason to fight. The enemy was informed that the Aztecs were declaring war, and the two sides would agree to a place and time to meet.

Before leaving for battle, all warriors performed autosacrifice to ask the gods to grant them victory. Priests carrying images of the deities left for the battlefield first, marching a day ahead of the warriors. Enemy troops met the Aztec army outside the enemy city. The meeting was loud, as both sides shouted, beat drums, and blew whistles, horns, and flutes. At a signal, both sides began the attack.

At first, the two armies remained about 200 feet (60 m) apart. Archers sent arrows flying into the enemy's ranks, while slingers flung rocks at the opposing forces. After a few minutes, the

Today, painting one's body to resemble a jaguar is reserved for ceremonial dances, not war.

arrows and rocks were used up, and the two sides moved closer together, until shorter-range weapons such as dart-throwers could be used. A couple minutes later, the soldiers moved in for hand-to-hand combat. Although many soldiers were killed in this manner, the goal was to capture an enemy soldier alive. Killing the enemy was considered careless and wasteful, since the enemy soldier could have been offered as a sacrifice to the gods. Wounding the enemy in order to make his capture easier was allowed, though. Throughout the fighting, the most experienced warriors made up the front lines, while young soldiers remained toward the back. At times, the Aztecs used battlefield strategy to overcome their enemies. They might pretend to retreat, only to lure their opponents into an ambush of additional troops.

A battle ended when one side retreated or surrendered. It could also end if the attacker was able to access the enemy city and set its temple on fire as a signal of victory. Most Aztec wars consisted of only one large battle. Although a defeated city was forced to pay tribute to Tenochtitlan, the Aztecs usually allowed the tlatoani of the city-state to remain in power. However, if a tlatoani fought until the very end and refused to surrender, he might be sacrificed and replaced by a tlatoani of the emperor's choosing.

After a war, victorious Aztec warriors returned home to cheering crowds and the music of drums and horns made of shells. Successful warriors were given gifts of food, chocolate, and jewelry such as ear and lip plugs. Those who had taken captives were promoted to new ranks. On the rare occasions when they met defeat, the soldiers wept as they entered the city of Tenochtitlan.

Hand-to-hand combat could result in many casualties, which Aztecs tried to avoid.

THE MACEHUALTIN MAJORITY

The majority of people in the Aztec Empire were not born into noble families. They were macehualtin, or commoners. Levels of wealth varied greatly among individuals in this class, which encompassed farmers, artisans, and merchants. Regardless of their wealth, all commoners served the nobles by providing tribute payments as well as labor service. Commoners were called upon to build temples, canals, and other public works.

Most commoners were peasant farmers who worked lands controlled by nobles. Those who lived near the mountains built **terraces** on the hillsides to create fields. Farmers living in Tenochtitlan or along the shores of the nearby lakes created *chinampas* for their

Mexican painter Diego Rivera imagined a bustling market scene in his mural of Tlatelolco.

crops. These fields were built by pounding wooden stakes into the lakebed and then building underwater "walls" of vines or branches between the stakes. The resulting enclosure was filled with soil dug from the lake bottom until it created an island standing about three feet (0.9 m) above the surface of the lake. Willow trees were planted along the edge of a chinampa to help anchor the land to the lakebed. Then crops such as maize, tomatoes, beans, and chilis were planted.

From May until November, most farmers spent long days working in their fields. During the rest of the year, however, many worked as part-time artisans. They created items for everyday use, such as pottery, sandals, brooms, stone tools, rope, and cloth. They sold these goods in the market.

In contrast to everyday goods, luxury items for the nobility were produced by full-time artisans known as *tolteca*. Among the most important tolteca were the feather workers. Feathers were the most valuable objects in the Aztec Empire,

treasured even above gold. Feather workers fashioned them into elaborate designs on such things as shields, clothing, headdresses, and wall hangings.

The tolteca also included goldsmiths, jewelers, painters, and sculptors. The position of these artisans was generally hereditary, with sons training as *apprentices* under their fathers. Most tolteca lived in cities, where they could easily get their goods to nobles. Some worked in the home of the emperor or a tlatoani and produced goods for him. Others worked as independent artisans, producing items at the request of individual nobles. Tolteca also sold some of their items in the market.

Nearly every city and town in the empire had its own market. The smallest markets were held only once or twice a month, but those in larger cities were held weekly. Some specialized in certain goods such as jewels, feathers, obsidian, dogs, honey, or slaves.

The largest market was located in the city of Tlatelolco on the same island as Tenochtitlan. It was open daily and drew crowds of up to 60,000

Aztec documents were usually recorded on long sheets of a kind of paper called *amatl*.

Did You Know?

AZTEC NOBLES PLAYED

A BALL GAME CALLED

tlachtli; THE RESULTS

OF THE GAME WERE

OFTEN USED IN

PREDICTING THE

FUTURE, WITH EACH

TEAM REPRESENTING A

CERTAIN PREDICTION.

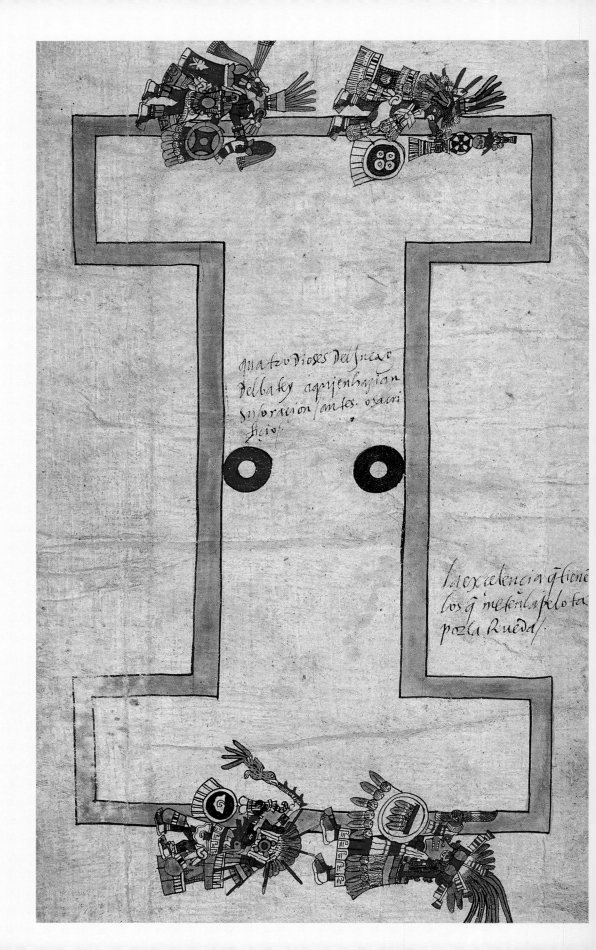

people. Tlatelolco's market sold every item imaginable. There were foods, live animals, jewels, gold and silver objects, bones, shells, feathers, pottery, animal skins, and more.

Each type of good was offered in its own area of the market. Goods were usually spread out on mats on the ground, and the sellers called out prices to shoppers. The Aztecs did not use money. Instead, goods were worth a certain number of **cacao beans** (for inexpensive items) or cotton cloaks (for luxury goods).

Goods were brought to Tlatelolco's market across the causeways leading into the city or by canoe. At any given time, there may have been 50,000 or more canoes on the lakes surrounding the island. Canals allowed the boats to bring goods right to the market. Some goods—especially those made by artisans—were sold by those who had produced them. Merchants sold other items. Often, a merchant specialized in a specific item, such as salt. Some merchants traveled to regional markets to sell their goods.

Other, more elite, merchants known as *pochteca* traveled to markets even farther away. They spent months at a time on trading expeditions, often venturing outside the borders of the Aztec Empire. Pochteca traded in luxury goods, including feathers, gold, necklaces, and **coral**. Often, pochteca were called upon to serve as spies for the empire as well. They gathered information about an enemy's army and defense capabilities.

Pochteca were richly rewarded for their efforts. They were at the top of the commoner class and under some emperors were even allowed some of the privileges of the nobility, including the right to wear noble clothing for ceremonies, to own land, and to sacrifice slaves. The riches they collected on their expeditions made them wealthier than many nobles. The position of a pochteca was usually hereditary.

No matter what their future occupation, boys and girls from commoner families began to attend school at a telpochcalli around the age of 10, although the most promising youths were often sent to a calmecac. Boys and girls were taught separately at the telpochcalli, but both learned ritual singing, dancing, and music-making. Boys also worked on construction projects and trained to become warriors. Girls focused on housekeeping.

Like noblewomen, female commoners generally married young. Once she had married, a common woman spent her days spinning, weaving, and cleaning. Women also did the family's shopping at the market, and some served as vendors to sell their family's wares. Meal preparation fell to women, too, and they might spend up to five hours a day grinding corn to make tortillas and tamales. They rarely prepared meat, which was too expensive.

Commoner families lived in one-story homes

Like other ball games in Mesoamerica, tlachtli was played on a court with a narrow alley.

made of adobe or stone. Most homes had only one or two rooms, although the homes of the pochteca and other wealthy commoners might be larger. No matter the size, all homes had an *altar*, where the family worshiped and kept small statues of various gods.

The homes of commoners were generally grouped into neighborhoods known as *calpulli*. In some cases, the residents of a calpulli belonged to the same profession. Other calpulli contained residents from several different occupations. Each calpulli had its own patron deity, temple, and school.

Although most commoners were not wealthy, they generally had enough to provide food and shelter for their family. During years of famine or hardship, however, some commoners sold themselves into slavery. People might also become slaves if they were in debt or committed a crime. No one was born into slavery; even the child of a slave was born free. Although slaves were not paid for their work, they were given shelter and food. They were able to marry and own property. Slave masters owned only the work that the slaves performed. That work usually involved products made from spinning or weaving or overseeing the land and management of the master's estate. Slaves could eventually buy their freedom, or they could be freed at a temple or palace.

After being freed, a slave returned to his or her former social status as a commoner. All commoners could move up within their class by making outstanding achievements in war, as a priest, or in trade or craft-making. But, because of their birth, commoners could never achieve full equality with the noble class. Under certain emperors, the rights of high-ranking commoners were expanded, however. In the mid-1400s, the emperor Moctezuma I created the office of *quauhpilli*, or "eagle lord" to reward the most successful commoner warrior with some of the privileges of the nobility. By the early 1500s, however, Moctezuma II had abolished the title of the eagle lord and even denied promising commoner children access to the calmecac, leaving Aztec society more divided than ever.

Did You Know?

FOR TRADE, A COTTON CLOAK WAS WORTH UP TO 100 CACAO BEANS. AN AVOCADO MIGHT COST ONLY 3 CACAO BEANS, WHILE A NECKLACE COULD COST 600 CLOAKS.

Markets typically formed around a city's temples, as that was the center of all activity.

ECHOES OF THE AZTEC

By the beginning of the 16th century, the Aztec Empire reached to lands more than 620 miles (998 km) from the capital. Ruling such a vast empire became increasingly difficult. Many city-states were angered by the Aztecs' constant demands for tribute. In addition, with more than 3 million people in the empire, food shortages became common.

Despite such difficulties, the Aztec Empire might have continued to flourish for many years. But in 1519, a Spanish **conquistador** named Hernán Cortés arrived in Tenochtitlan. He and the soldiers with him were astounded by the city's wealth—and they wanted it for themselves. The Spanish recruited 70,000 native troops eager to be free of Aztec domination to join them in a

The Spanish captured Cuauhtémoc, the last Aztec emperor, in 1521 and killed him in 1525.

war against Tenochtitlan. The Spaniards' firearms—as well as the diseases they unknowingly introduced to the local population—proved too much for the Aztec. The last Aztec emperor, Cuauhtémoc, was captured on August 13, 1521. The Aztec Empire was at an end.

Immediately after their victory, the Spanish began to rule the lands once held by the Aztecs. They built their capital, Mexico City, over the ruins of Tenochtitlan. Spanish rulers provided grants of land to the many Spaniards who settled in the area. Aztecs were required to work these lands in a system known as the encomienda (Spanish for "commission" or "charge"). Under the encomienda, the Spaniards made up the new upper class. Some Aztec nobles, such as the tlatoque, retained their positions, although they were now under the authority of the Spaniards.

Although parts of the Aztec culture were lost in the years after the Spanish conquest, much of

it was incorporated into the new Spanish—and later Mexican—culture. No full-blooded Aztec descendants remain today, but many of the people of Mexico have some Aztec heritage. And more than one million of them still speak the Aztec language, Nahuatl. In addition, Aztec religious beliefs were incorporated into the *Christianity* that the Spaniards spread throughout much of Mexico.

Although many Aztec sites have been built over, archaeologists continue to dig for clues to the Aztec past. Some of the most amazing finds, including the Templo Mayor, have been dug up from beneath the streets of Mexico City. These buildings—along with writings from the Aztec period—give scholars a picture of a strictly divided society in which each person had his or her own place. But everyone came together to form the rich culture now known as the Aztec Empire.

Descendants of the Aztecs continue to celebrate the ancient culture in the present day.

c. 950	—	The Toltecs dominate the Valley of Mexico but lose power by about 1150.
c. 1100	—	The Mexica begin to migrate south from their homeland.
c. 1250	—	The Mexica enter the Valley of Mexico and settle temporarily in various places.
c. 1325	—	The Mexica settle permanently on an island in Lake Texcoco and found the city of Tenochtitlan.
c. 1355	—	The Mexica ally themselves with the Tepanecs, providing tribute in return for protection.
c. 1355	—	The market city of Tlatelolco is founded on the same island as Tenochtitlan.
1375	—	The Mexica appoint their first tlatoani.
1428	—	The Mexica overcome the Tepanecs and form the Triple Alliance, or Aztec Empire, with Texcoco and Tlacopan.
1428	—	The emperor Itzcoatl destroys books from city-states in the Valley of Mexico and rewrites history to glorify the Mexica.
1440	—	Moctezuma I becomes emperor.
1450	—	A four-year drought affects Aztec lands.
1454	—	An extensive expansion project is begun on the Templo Mayor.
1454	—	Famine leads many Aztecs to sell themselves into slavery.
1487	—	The renovated Templo Mayor is dedicated with massive human sacrifices.
1502	—	Floods cover much of Tenochtitlan.
1502	—	Moctezuma II becomes emperor.
1518	—	Reports of foreigners in Mexico reach Moctezuma II.
1519	—	Hernán Cortés arrives on the Mexican coast and marches to Tenochtitlan.
1520	—	Moctezuma II is killed.
1521	—	The Aztec Empire is defeated by the Spanish and their native allies.

ADOBE: a building material made from straw and clay dried in the sun

ALTAR: a special table used for carrying out religious rituals

APPRENTICES: people who learn a job or craft by working under the guidance of someone with more experience

CACAO BEANS: the seeds of an evergreen tree native to South America that are used to make chocolate

CAUSEWAYS: raised roadways, often built across water

CHRISTIANITY: a religion based on the teachings and person of Jesus of Nazareth; it professes that Jesus is the son of God, that he died for the sins of all people, and that he rose from the dead

CONQUISTADOR: the leader of a group of Spanish soldiers who took over lands in much of Mexico, Central America, and Peru during the 16th century

CORAL: the skeleton of tiny sea creatures called coral polyps; as the coral polyps die, the skeleton hardens into a rocklike substance that was used to make jewelry and other goods

FASTING: going without food

GLYPHS: symbols or pictures that stand for a certain idea, word, or sound in a writing system

MAGUEY: a plant with long, thick, spiny leaves that was used to make fiber for clothing as well as alcoholic drinks

MYTHOLOGY: a set of stories or beliefs, often about a society's gods, history, or ancestors

OBSIDIAN: a hard, dark rock made from cooled lava

PATRONS: special protectors or supporters

PLATEAU: a high, flat area of land

SCRIBES: people who were taught to read and write and were often employed in keeping records

TAMALES: foods made from cornmeal wrapped around meat or beans and steamed in corn husks

TERRACES: flat ridges built into the side of a hill to allow for farming

TRIBUTE: a payment made by a weaker nation to a stronger one, often as a result of conquest or for protection

TUNICS: knee-length, loose-fitting shirts

Selected Bibliography

Aguilar-Moreno, Manuel. *Handbook to Life in the Aztec World*. New York: Oxford University Press, 2007.

Boone, Elizabeth Hill. *The Aztec World*. Washington, D.C.: Smithsonian, 1994.

Burland, Cottie, and Werner Forman. *The Aztecs: Gods and Fate in Ancient Mexico*. New York: Galahad, 1980.

Carrasco, Davíd, and Scott Sessions. *Daily Life of the Aztecs: People of the Sun and Earth*. Westport, Conn.: Greenwood Press, 1998.

Conrad, Geoffrey W., and Arthur A. Demarest. *Religion and Empire: The Dynamics of Aztec and Inca Expansionism*. New York: Cambridge University Press, 1984.

Saunders, Nicholas J. *Ancient Americas: Maya, Aztec, Inka & Beyond*. Gloucestershire, UK: Sutton, 2004.

Smith, Michael E. *The Aztecs*. Malden, Mass.: Blackwell, 1996.

Van Tuerenhout, Dirk R. *The Aztecs: New Perspectives*. Santa Barbara, Calif.: ABC-CLIO, 2005.

Websites

AZTECS

http://www.history.com/topics/aztecs

Watch related videos and learn more about Aztec and Mexican history from the History Channel's website.

PBS: CONQUISTADORS—THE FALL OF THE AZTECS

http://www.pbs.org/conquistadors/cortes/cortes_flat.html

Learn more about how Hernán Cortés and his army brought an end to the Aztec Empire.

Note: Every effort has been made to ensure that the websites listed above are suitable for children, that they have educational value, and that they contain no inappropriate material. However, because of the nature of the Internet, it is impossible to guarantee that these sites will remain active indefinitely or that their contents will not be altered.